Raps, Riddles and Concrete

Pie Corbett

Chrysalis Children's Books

First published in the UK in 2005 by
Chrysalis Children's Books
An imprint of Chrysalis Books Group Plc
The Chrysalis Building, Bramley Road
London W10 6SP

ISBN 1 84458 187 X

British Library Cataloguing in Publication
Data for this book is available from the
British Library.

Associate publisher: Joyce Bentley
Editor and project manager: Nicola Edwards
Designers: Rachel Hamdi, Holly Mann
Illustrators: Serena Curmi, Ed Eaves,
Andrea Huseinovic, Maddy McClellan,
Kate Pankhurst, Melanie Sharp, Woody

Printed in China

10 9 8 7 6 5 4 3 2 1

Contents

About this book

"**Hello**. My name is Pie Corbett (yes, I know – silly name, isn't it?). If, like me, you enjoy writing poetry – or even if you think you don't – then this is the book for you! In it you will find lots of ideas and examples to help you with your writing. You won't need much else – just a pencil, a notebook and plenty of imagination. Everyone dreams, everyone wonders 'what would happen if….' – and that is using your imagination!

Some of the poems in this book are all about looking closely at the world around you and being aware of your senses.

I'll show you how you can use a few poetic techniques to capture forever what you saw and how you felt.

Several of the poems are more about playing with ideas and words. Some have a form to follow – a repeating pattern or a rhyming pattern. For each type of poem I'll give you an example and then show you step by step how you can write your own version. If you find this hard at first, do not worry – your writing will get better with practice. Just write what you want to write, then read back through your poem. Check that you've chosen the best words to help your poem say what you really want it to say."

How to use the book

A poem I've written or one I remember from when I was at school

Poem technique featured

My ideas about the poem

A step-by-step guide to writing your own poem

Tips to help you with writing or performing your poems

More ideas for creating similar types of poem

Use the chart on page 5 to find out about the poems included in the book and the poetic techniques they feature. The chart also lists well-known examples of the same types of poem.

Poem	Type	Features	Other examples
Ten Tiny Tales	Counting rhyme	Alliteration	One, Two, Buckle my Shoe – anon.
Secret Wishes	Patterned list poem	Repetition Word play Adjectives	Stars – Carl Sandburg
City Café	Patterned list poem	Senses Close observation Well-chosen words	First Robin – Jane Yolen
The Motorbike	Free verse	Similes (like) Close observation Alliteration Well-chosen adjectives	Thistles – Ted Hughes
Alien Feelings	Patterned list poem Alphabet poem	Similes (as...as)	An Alphabet of Horrible Habits – Colin West
Shadow Rain Summer Ice	Shape poems Concrete poems Thin poems Calligrams	Word play Alliteration Well-chosen words	Giant Rocket – Wes Magee
The School Blues	Nonsense poetry Humorous poem	Swapping words Word play	I Went to the Pictures Tomorrow – anon.
Humpty's Journey Spongee Mung Sparg	Nonsense poetry Nursery rhymes Rhyming verse	Inventing nonsense words Rhythm	Jabberwocky – Lewis Carroll
I am the Grouchosaurus	Free verse	Similes Comparisons	The Jumblies – Edward Lear
Empty City The Meeting Loneliness	Haiku	Senses Powerful words Syllables	Haiku – Basho
Not Last Night	Rhyming verse Counting rhyme Couplets	Rhyme Rhythm	Not Last Night – but the Night Before – anon.
School Daze Rap	Performance poetry Rap Rhyming verse	Patterned rhyme Rhythm Syllables	Patchwork Rap – Adrian Mitchell

Ten Tiny Tales

One white worm wiggled
wildly while whistling.

Six serious salads sat silently
on a squashy sofa.

Two terrifying tigers
tap-danced on a table.

Seven silly spiders stood
on seven sad stools.

Three thirsty thieves
threw thirty thin thorns.

Eight apes ate eighty
ancient acorns.

Four fine foxes fetched
a fearful fish.

Nine naughty newts
nibbled a nervous nut.

Five famous ferrets found
fourteen flabby frogs.

Ten tired toes taught two
tangled turtles to tango.

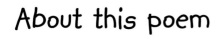

About this poem

" I had a lot of fun writing this poem.
Using numbers made it easy to build the poem.
But I also had to try to find lots of words that
started with the same sound! "

Over to you

To write your own counting poem, first you need to write
the numbers one to ten down one side of the page.
Then think of something that starts with the same sound
as each number. Using words that start with the same sound
is called 'alliteration'. It helps to make lines memorable.

One whale...   Two tigers...

Next add in a describing word (an adjective).

One wet whale...   Two tiny tigers...

Then say what is happening (add a verb).

One wet whale walked...
Two tiny tigers talked...

If you can, make your lines longer.

One wet whale walked wisely
to windy Washington.

Two tiny tigers talked to
ten tired turkeys.

Writing tip

✰ It's good to get into the habit
of rereading your poems to see if there
are places where you can improve
them. For example, in the poem on p6,
my first line started like this:

**One white worm went along
while whistling.**

I thought the word 'went' was a bit
weak because it did not show the
reader how the worm was moving,
so I changed it to:

**One white worm wiggled wildly
while whistling.**

7

Secret Wishes

I wish I could capture
a sizzling sunbeam
and hide it under my pillow.

I wish I could capture
unkind words
and keep them like wasps
buzzing in a bag.

I wish I could capture
a quiver of lightning
and use it to power
my memory bank
when the battery is low.

I wish I could capture
the sound of snow falling
like white moths' wings beating
to soften angry thoughts.

I wish I could capture
the feel of my cat's fur
and the sound of her purr.

I wish I could capture
a cool raindrop
and let it quieten my thoughts
as the poem ends.

About this poem

" I often wonder what would happen if I was granted three magical wishes! In this poem I made some wonderful wishes. Look back at how I repeated the same pattern over and over again to make a structure for my poem. "

Over to you

You could write your own patterned poem, using the opening words 'I dreamed I saw'. First add on an idea:

I dreamed I saw a snake.

Next add an adjective to give some description:

I dreamed I saw a thin snake.

Now add a verb to say what it is doing:

I dreamed I saw a thin snake
gliding through the grass.

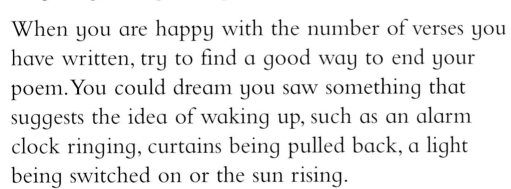

When you are happy with the number of verses you have written, try to find a good way to end your poem. You could dream you saw something that suggests the idea of waking up, such as an alarm clock ringing, curtains being pulled back, a light being switched on or the sun rising.

Writing tip

✰ Try including some alliteration in your poem, e.g. **Buzzing in a bag...**
White moths' wings....

More ideas

You could also try using one of these openings to start a different list poem:

If only I could...

Have you seen...

This is the day when...

City Café

I like to look at
The distant tower block
Like a giant's finger.

I like to listen to
The fast cars cruising
Down the road.

I like to touch
The cool, cold glass of milk.

I like to sniff
The scent of coffee
Drifting from the café.

I like to taste
The sweet crunch
Of a hot doughnut.

I like to dream
Of distant castles
And dangerous dragons.

About this poem

 I wrote this poem on a hot, sunny day. I was sitting outside a café and watching the world go by. To help me write the poem, I used a simple pattern – and all my senses. Describing what you can see, hear, touch, smell and taste helps to bring your world alive for your readers. "

Over to you

You can use your senses to create a poem of your own. Take your notebook to a place that you like, such as your local park.

Write down a few things that you can see.

> trees

Make a note of any sounds you can hear.

> bees buzzing

Can you smell, touch or taste anything special?

> a dog's fur

Borrow my pattern to help write your poem. Take your ideas and add some words around them, e.g.

> I like to look at the old trees
> bending in the wind
> like old men.

 **Writing tip**

✧ Try to use interesting words. Look at this sentence:

The dog came down the road.

It is rather dull. We can make it more interesting by using more precise nouns and more powerful verbs, and adding description:

The eager puppy raced down the shady lane.

The Motorbike

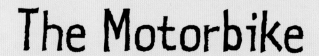

It leans at the roadside
Waiting for its owner to return.

The silver handles jut out
Like a cow's horns,
Ready for the biker's grip.

Black tyres whirl round.
The silver wheels spin
Like bright suns.
Spokes spring
From the centre
Like a fan.

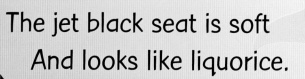

The jet black seat is soft
And looks like liquorice.

It growls down the street,
Like an angry dog;
The back light is like a red eye.

The biker boy sits back,
Lets the breeze take him.

About this poem

" Before writing this poem I looked carefully at a
motorbike and made notes about what I could see.
I tried to choose descriptive words, and used
alliteration and similes. A simile is where you say
that one thing is like another. For instance,
'the moon is like a banana' is a simile. Can you
find the similes in my motorbike poem? "

Over to you

To write your own observation poem, you must choose
something to write about that really interests you. It might
be a type of car or a tree or anything else – it's up to you.
First you need to look at the object carefully.

leaves

The tree

Write down what you can see.
Drawing it can help.
Add descriptive words and ideas.

branches

The tall trunk towers high.

trunk

Try using a simile to describe your object.
Think about what it looks like. What does it remind you of?

The tall trunk towers high
like an elephant's leg.

Set out your poem on the page
– you can use long and short lines.

The tall trunk
towers high
like an elephant's leg.

 Writing tip

✦ Using a simile helps to build a
picture in the reader's mind. It
describes what something looks like:

I saw a snake sliding through the
sand like an eel through water.

Alien Feelings

Sometimes I feel –

As **angry** as an alien lost in outer space,
As **blue** as an alien hidden in a cloudless sky,
As **cool** as an alien sleeping in the freezer,
As **dreadful** as a three-headed alien with three thumping headaches,
As **energetic** as an alien in an Olympic final,
As **famous** as an alien movie star,
As **greedy** as an alien eating three breakfasts,
As **happy** as an alien watching a jelly on telly,
As **idle** as an alien with nothing to do,
As **jumpy** as an alien on a kangaroo,
As **kind** as an alien who thinks it is your birthday every day...

About this poem

" In this poem I used lots of examples of a special sort of simile built around the word 'as'. They helped me to describe how I feel. Sometimes I feel like an alien. Maybe I came from another planet? "

Over to you

You can use similes to build a picture in your readers' minds. For example, using the simile 'as thin as a leaf' helps to describe how thin something is. To write your moody poem, first make a list of your 'alien' moods:

> angry, excited, happy,
> lively, lonely, sad...

Now use a simile to describe each mood:

> As angry as an alien chased by a wasp...
> As happy as an alien chewing a chocolate bar...
> As lonely as an alien abandoned on an asteroid...

When you reread your poem, always look out for places where you could improve it. Sometimes you can do this by changing a word to make it more powerful, expressive or more precise. For example,

> As angry as an alien
> chased by a bird

sounds weak because the word 'bird' is too vague. What sort of bird? Was it an eagle or an emu? An ostrich or a penguin?

Writing tip

✫ Can you *see* how I have used the alphabet to help structure my poem? I started the second word in each line (in this case an adjective) with the next letter of the alphabet. The alphabet can be very handy for providing a structure – though beware! Some letters are hard to find a word for!

SHADOW

Snapping

at my heel

-- my faithful twin.

RAIN

Again
and
again,
the
rain
silently
slips
down
the
window
pane,
again
and
again.

SUMMER ICE

The cold bite
Of sweet ice;
A sudden
c r u s h
Of stars
B e t w e e n
t
e
e
t
h

About these poems

> I love playing with words on the page because you can draw with them! A shape or concrete poem uses words to make shapes on the page that add to the impact of the poem. Sometimes they are in the shape of the poem's subject.

Over to you

There are lots of ways to make shapes out of poems.

'Thin' poems Try writing a 'thin' poem – where the words run down the page. This would be good for writing about anything that reminds you of a thin line, such as rain falling, a blade of grass, a rope, Rapunzel's hair, a tree or a waterfall.

Calligrams To create a calligram, write a word and use your handwriting to make the letters suggest the meaning. So, the word 'shaky' would be written with wobbly letters, like this: 'shaky'
The word 'shadow' would have a shadow.

Shape poems To make a shape poem, write about an object and then arrange the words to form a picture of the object. A shape poem about the sun, might look like this:

Beware – I am a golden coin – but too hot to touch!

Writing tip

☆ Remember – you can use alliteration and similes in your concrete poems. Choose your words with care. See if you can:

1. Use stronger words – 'beagle' rather than 'dog'.

2. Add in extra description – 'the golden coin' rather than 'the coin'.

The School Blues

I smiled up this morning
With a woke on my face.

I climbed out of my teeth,
Brushed downstairs
And ran bed.

I ate my street,
Had a glass of bus
And ran down the breakfast
To catch the school milk.

The bus passed through the school gates,
Jogged cars and buses,
Greeted shops and lights
Till we reached the city streets.

I waited lessons
And *dashed* into quietly
For the school to begin.

About this poem

"I have never liked getting out of bed in the morning. So I decided that I would change getting up in the morning to make it more exciting. I had fun writing this nonsense poem. Can you see how I did it?"

Over to you

Create a crazy day poem of your own. First, write down a description of how you get to school or what you do in school.

This morning we poured all the paint into pots
and laid them on the table.

Now swap some of the words around.
Try doing this in different ways:

This paint we poured all the morning into the table
and laid them on pots.

This morning we laid all the paint into pots
and poured them on the table.

Once you have decided which words to swap, you can set the sentences out into a shape:

This paint we poured all the morning into the table and laid them on pots.

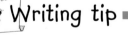

Writing tip

☆ Look back at your finished poem. You may find that you have *been* swapping over certain word types to make your new sentences. For example, I often swap the verbs over: I brushed upstairs and ran my hair. Sometimes I swap over the nouns: The milk opened the cat and knocked over the fridge. Swapping the adjectives also works well: I sipped the sweltering milk while the icy sun blazed down.

Humpty's Journey

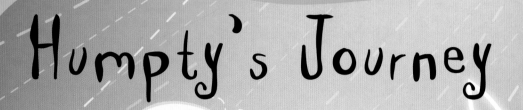

Humpty Dumpty sat on a train.
Humpty Dumpty got caught in the rain.

He tried to get dry and he tried to get warm.
But it's not that easy in a thunderstorm.

Spongee Mung Sparg

The grouches are in the spongee. The sparg are in the mungee. The slobod are in the scrob. The chumps are in the shlob.

About these poems

" It is great fun to take a rhyme that you know well and alter it. In the first poem, I wrote my own version of 'Humpty Dumpty'. Did you spot that the second poem is also based on a nursery rhyme? I kept the same pattern and beat but made up some nonsense words. Can you recognize the nursery rhyme? (It helps if you chant it aloud to hear the rhythm.) "

Over to you

To write your own poem based on a nursery rhyme, first of all choose a rhyme that you know really well. I find it helps to write the rhyme down.

Jack and Jill went up the hill
To fetch a pail of water;
Jack fell down and broke his crown
And Jill came tumbling after.

Now start to make some changes! For example, you could change the names of the characters, where they went and why:

Sam and Jo went down to town
To buy a brand new house...

When you are thinking about what changes to make, remember that you have to keep the same rhyming pattern, like this:

Sam slipped over in a field of clover
And Jo sat down by a mouse!

More ideas

My second poem is based on 'Little Boy Blue'. Did you recognize it? To have some fun with nonsense words is not that hard. First, write out some lines of a nursery rhyme, e.g.

The cows are in the meadow,
The sheep are in the corn.

Then make up some invented words. To do this you could write a list of words, e.g. action, supply, running, book. Then swap endings around, e.g. actook, supption, runnly, booing. Now swap some words from the rhyme for invented ones, like this:

The supption are in the runnly,
The booing are in the actook.

I Am the Grouchosaurus

My head is bigger than a bus
And my eyes shine like headlamps.

My hair hangs down like slimy spaghetti
And my skin is tougher than an elephant's hide.

My hands are like metallic clamps
And my body is made of metal girders
Stolen from the Eiffel Tower.

I don't eat meat or plants.
I eat the metal parts of machines
And the silvery hearts of computers.

I don't walk on legs
But I stride across the city
On steel struts.

When I speak,
The storm clouds clash.
But no one answers.
For where my heart should be
Is an empty TV set…

About this poem

" The great thing about poetry is that you can make anything you like. I wondered what it might be like to be a monster! I asked myself: What would it look like? What sounds could it make? What could it do? "

Over to you

Try drawing your D.I.Y. monster before writing about it. Drawing is a good way to help your imagination develop ideas. Think about the face, the eyes, the body, the hands, the legs – try borrowing bits from other objects or creatures so that you assemble your monster from lots of different parts!

You can use my sentence starters to build your poem or make up some of your own. Then just add your ideas. Remember to use powerful similes to create a picture of your monster in your readers' minds.

I am the...
My head is...
And my eyes...

More ideas

You can use comparisons to make riddles to puzzle your friends. First of all, think of a subject for your riddle. Jot down everything you know about what you want to describe – what it does, looks like, sounds like and how it is used. Then make up some clues. Using similes can help. Here are some 'one line' riddles:

1. What is sometimes blue but you cannot swim in it?
2. What is white and fluffy but never bleats?
3. What is hotter than curry, warmer than toast but too far away to touch?

Answers: 1.the sky 2. clouds 3. the sun

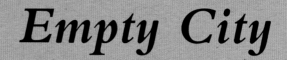

Empty City

The silver moon glistens.
Streets are empty.
A siren howls.

The Meeting

The scattered stars glitter.
A fox pauses.
Cars growl.

Loneliness

The shops are shut.
Doorways stay empty
Though someone snores.

About these poems

> I love writing haiku. They are fun to write because they are so small – like miniature poems. The Japanese invented haiku and they were originally written onto a painting of a scene. Most haiku are set in a season – summer, winter, autumn or spring. Usually they are to do with nature.

Over to you

In a haiku you try to take a snapshot of a scene, capturing a special moment. Most haiku are three lines long – but you could write haiku of one, two, three or four lines – it's up to you!

Look carefully at how I have written my haiku. I began by thinking of a memorable scene, such as my garden at night.

The first line is something that I can see in my scene:

> The scattered stars glitter.

The second line is something else I can see:

> A fox pauses.

The third line is something I can hear:

> Cars growl.

Notice how I tried to choose my words carefully and use powerful language: scattered, glitter, pauses, growl.

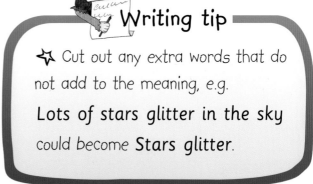

Writing tip

★ Cut out any extra words that do not add to the meaning, e.g.

Lots of stars glitter in the sky could become **Stars glitter.**

NOT LAST NIGHT

Late last night,
Not the night before,
Twenty four robbers
Came knocking at my door.

I went downstairs to let them in
And this is what I saw –

Number one was a hairy gnome,
Number two was afar from home.

Number three was tall and fair,
Number four had ginger hair.

Number five was a man of truth,
Number six held a horse's hoof.

Number seven was my best friend,
Number eight went round the bend.

Number nine was dressed in black,
So number ten took him back.

About this poem

" You might be wondering why I haven't mentioned rhyme yet. Well, it is not easy to use. I based my rhyming poem on an old playground rhyme. "

Over to you

When you use rhyme there's a risk that you will lose what you want to say and end up with nonsense instead. For example, imagine I wanted to start a poem with the line

The trees blew hard in the storm.

If I wanted the next line to rhyme, I would have to find a rhyme for the word 'storm'. But if I could only think of one rhyming word, I might have to continue my poem like this:

The trees blew hard in the storm.
I was in my uniform.

It doesn't make much sense, does it? That is why it is easiest to use rhyme in nonsense poems, where the sound of the words is more important than what they mean.

In your poem, try using the same number pattern that I used. Practise writing rhyming couplets (pairs of lines that rhyme). Try to get the right rhythm (beat) to the lines.

Writing tip

☆ It helps to chant each pair of lines out loud to hear if each line follows the same pattern. The lines should have the same number of beats – one should not be longer than the other. Listen carefully to the beat of the words to see if each line sounds right. It might help to tap out the rhythm while you say the lines.

To help you think of words that rhyme, the alphabet can be useful.

back crack   hack lack   pack rack tack yak
a b c d e f g h i j k l m n o p q r s t u v w x y z
black flak   Jack knack   quack sack whack

School Daze Rap

Hip hop hap
It's the school daze rap.
Clap – clap – clappetty – clap.

Not so cool –

We're in school –

Sitting still –

I'm no fool.

Hip hop hap
It's the school daze rap.
Clap – clap – clappetty – clap.

Teachers talk –

Numbers fly –

Get it wrong –

Have to try.

Hip hop hap
It's the school daze rap.
Clap – clap – clappetty – clap.

Reading books –
All the time –
Passing looks –
Is a crime.

Hip hop hap
It's the school daze rap.
Clap – clap – clappetty – clap.

About this poem

" I love performing my poems. Rhyming poems with plenty of rhythm sound good read aloud. Have a go at performing this rap – use the tips on this page to help you. Try reading it forwards and backwards. "

Over to you

When you write a rap, it can be useful to think of the chorus before working out the verses. You need a chorus between each verse. It helps to make the rap sound like a song. You could borrow my chorus or make up one of your own.

Hip hop hap
It's the school daze rap.
Clap – clap – clappetty – clap.

When you write each verse, make sure there are the same number of beats in each line. Say the words in my verses and you will notice that each line has only three beats:

1	2	3
Teach	ers	talk –
Num	bers	fly –
Get	it	wrong –
Have	to	try.

Try to keep to the same rhyming pattern as my rap. I have rhymed the second and fourth line of each verse.

Writing tip

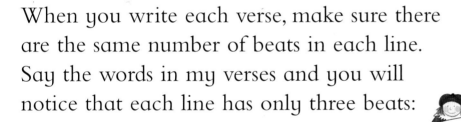

☆ Try using a rhyming dictionary to help you find rhymes. If you get stuck for a rhyme – then change the line that you are trying to find a rhyme for! Keep saying the poem aloud to hear how it sounds.

Performing tips

☆ Keep the words loud and clear.

☆ Read with rhythm.

☆ Use expression.

☆ Record your voice to hear how you sound.

A Poet's Toolkit
Creating patterns and special effects

How to set your poem out

✫ Some poems use a pattern. This might mean that you repeat the same opening for each line:

I dreamed I saw a spaceship sleeping.
I dreamed I saw a blade
of grass weeping.

✫ Other poems are more like songs, with verses and a repeating chorus, like the rap on page 28:

Hip hop hap
It's the school daze rap.
Clap – clap – clappetty – clap.

✫ Sometimes you can use the shape of a poem to suggest its subject:

The snake slithers, slipping through the long grass, leaving even my hands trembling.

✫ Other poems have no real shape but make their own pattern on the page. You can use short or long lines:

Sunlight glows
In the back yard
Warming the stones –
The distant traffic
Grumbles...

Two things that you can do in a poem

1. You can play with ideas and create something nonsensical:

I dreamed that I saw a stone humming a tune.

2. You can also try to say what something is really like:

silver raindrops
tremble

How to use special effects

Poets have a few special effects that they use.
Here are my favourite ones that we have
looked at in this book:

- ✧ Make sure you choose
  good words:

  builds a stronger picture than

  The Siamese cat crept by

  The cat went by.

- ✧ Try some alliteration:

  The curious cat crept by.

- ✧ Use similes with 'like':

  The cat curled up like a question
  mark in my lap.

- ✧ Use similes with 'as … as ….':

  The cat's fur,
  As soft as velvet...

How to polish your poems

When you reread your poems, check to see if you
can improve them by strengthening the meaning, like this:

- ✧ Use stronger words:

  poppy rather than flower.

- ✧ Add in extra description:
  rather than

  the curved moon
  the moon.

- ✧ Use alliteration:

  the trembling tears...

- ✧ Use a simile:

  'like' or 'as...as'.

- ✧ Cut out unwanted words:
  sounds better than

  the weary traveller
  the tired, weary, old, ancient traveller.

Now show your poem to someone else
to see what they think of it.

Glossary A B C

adjective A word which describes a noun, e.g. a red car.

alliteration A few words that begin with the same sound, e.g. two tiny tigers told a turtle to tickle its toes.

calligram A picture poem made of letters that show the meaning of the poem.

concrete poem A shape poem where the words add to the meaning.

haiku A short type of Japanese poem – usually three lines long – that captures a moment.

noun A type of word that names something or someone. Try to use precise nouns, e.g. 'Mercedes' rather than 'car'.

rhyme A rhyme happens when words share the same end sound pattern, e.g. cog, dog, fog, log.

rhyming couplets Pairs of lines that rhyme.

rhythm The sounds a poem makes that give it a beat.

riddle A puzzle where the subject has to be guessed.

simile A special poetic effect that compares one thing to another by using 'like' or 'as…as'.

verb A 'doing' or 'being' word. Try to use 'powerful' verbs, e.g. 'dashed' rather than 'went'.

Index